Hymns from my Notebooks

The Psalms

REV JEFFREY B CHILDS

History and beginning of my hymn writing

Though I had written a handful of hymns (or poems) prior to my retirement as a pastor in the United Methodist Church, it was in the summer of 2019 that I seriously began writing hymns. After forty years of following the teachings of John Wesley, I began to follow the hymn writing of his brother Charles. In his lifetime Charles Wesley wrote over 6000 hymns. I thought that if I could write roughly one a day, I could accomplish the same goal in eighteen years. (To date I have written a little over 1600.) The hymns in this collection were written in the four months between June 28 and October 31, 2022.

How to use this book

First, read the psalm in whatever translation you prefer, then read the hymn that I wrote based on that psalm. Some of these are based on the entire psalm and others on just one verse as you see in my notation for each one. I would ask you to prayerfully meditate on what you have read and then write your own reflections on what all this psalm, and perhaps this hymn, say to you.

This book is dedicated to my parents,

Harold and Louise Childs,

who always believed in me.

Hymns from my Notebooks
The Psalms

Copyright © 2025 by Jeffrey B. Childs
No portion of this book may be reproduced in any form without written permission from the publisher or author, except as permitted by U.S. copyright law.

All Common Good Stories publications may be ordered through online booksellers, including www.Amazon.com or by contacting:

Common Good Stories
5164 Rt 89
Romulus, NY 14541
www.commongoodstories.com

Because of the dynamics of the Internet, any web addresses or links contained in this book may have changed since publication and may no longer be valid. The views expressed in this book are solely those of the author and do not necessarily reflect the views of the publisher. We acknowledge there are many theological perspectives when interpreting scripture; we honor those we do publish.

Cover image credit: Robin Blair

All rights reserved.

Some Things to Us Are Blessings
(Psalm 1.1)

Some things to us are blessings,

Others are not really.

Discover for yourself what brings,

Pure joy to you ideally.

Jesus offered the Beatitudes,

To help us think and see,

Beyond the world's vain attitudes,

What true blessings just might be.

People May Plot but God Is Sure
(Psalm 2.1)

People may plot but God is sure,

Enemies are big but God is bigger.

People may waver but God is secure.

Figures don't lie, but liars figure.

God blesses those who draw near,

Approaching the royal throne,

Near to God there is none to fear,

God has claimed us for God's own.

We give thanks to God today,

For all there is and what might be.

There is one thing that we can say,

We are blessed for all eternity.

Deliver Me, O Lord
(Psalm 3.1)

Deliver me, O Lord,

From all my enemies.

You are always adored,

For answering my pleas.

Morning, noon, or night,

You are always there,

Doing what is right,

Offering me care.

To you I do confess,

All my sins and wrongs.

By grace your servant bless,

I'll praise you with my songs.

Lord, Be Gracious and Hear My Prayer
(Psalm 4)

Lord, be gracious and hear my prayer,

My fears and pains with you I share.

Your tender mercies never cease,

In you alone I can find peace.

Lord, be gracious and hear my prayer,

When I call, you're always there.

I'm blessed knowing you're with me,

Your faithful servant I'll always be.

Lord, be gracious and hear my prayer,

When burdens are too much to bear,

I come to you and bare my soul,

My broken heart is again made whole.

Let All God's People Rejoice
(Psalm 5.11)

Let all God's people rejoice.

With heartfelt joy let's sing.

Together with one voice,

To God our praise we bring.

Give thanks for this new day,

That for us the Lord has made.

Come before God now and pray,

May homage to God be paid.

Hear, O Lord, our confessions,

We raise to your heavens above.

To you we make our professions,

Of our grateful undying love.

Be Gracious to Me, O Lord
(Psalm 6.2)

Be gracious to me, O Lord,

For I am in a dark place.

With all of life I'm bored,

So, I long to see your face.

Bring me into your presence.

Give me a holy shove.

Give to me the essence,

Of your undying love.

Help me not to be hateful,

For that I can sometimes be.

Help me to always be grateful,

For all that you've done for me.

I Will Sing Praise
(Psalm 7.17)

I will sing praise to the Lord most high,

The Lord who rules land, sea, and sky.

God whose name is above all names,

God of the storms, winds, and flames.

God, by the power of your might,

Guide us to always do what's right.

That we might perfectly praise you,

By all we say and all we do.

You are the Shepherd, and we are the flock,

Help us talk the talk and walk the walk.

We are blessed when we follow you,

Through all of life you guide us through.

O Lord, Our Lord
(Psalm 8.1)

O Lord, our Lord,

How majestic is your name.

We worship you,

Your majesty we proclaim.

O Lord, our Lord,

How wondrous are your blessings.

We sing your praise,

With gratitude your church sings.

O Lord, our Lord,

How empowering is your call,

To go and serve,

And proclaim your love to all.

Lord, I Will Tell
(Psalm 9.1)

Lord, I will tell of your glorious deeds.

I will sing praises to your name.

Your blessings grow like mustard seeds.

Your Good News I shall always proclaim.

I look at all you have created,

And give thanks for all you have done.

With joy I have participated,

In ministries that help someone

O Lord, You Hear the Cry of the Meek
(Psalm 10.17)

O Lord, you hear the cry of the meek,

To them you incline your ear.

Respond to all whom of you seek,

Your power to calm all fear.

O Lord, there are some who make things worse,

Your word they disobey.

They disbelieve and your name curse,

They just go their own way.

O Lord, do justice to the oppressed.

Make all things just and true.

May everyone by you be blessed,

For you, Lord, always see us through.

The Lord Is Righteous
(Psalm 11.7)

The Lord is righteous,

Loving righteous deeds.

We can do God's will,

By sewing God's seeds.

The Lord has called us,

To always be true,

Forever faithful,

In all that we do.

If we are righteous,

We will see God's face.

Faithfully watch for,

That right time and place.

The Promises of the Lord
(Psalm 12.6)

The promises of the Lord,

Our promises that come true.

From the One to be adored,

The One who always comes through.

In times of stress and tumult,

Our fervent prayers we share.

In times that are most difficult,

Our God is always there.

We rely on God each day,

For everything we need.

With faith in God we pray,

That God's will, will succeed.

How Long, O Lord
(Psalm 13)

How long, O Lord, must I wait?

How long must I bear pain in my heart?

On your response I await.

When will my salvation start?

From ancient days cries rang out,

To the Lord they lifted prayers.

They prayed to God without a doubt,

That salvation would be theirs.

They trusted in the Lord's love,

As they lifted up their voice.

Salvation would come from God above,

Their hearts would again rejoice.

There Is No God, Only Fools Say
(Psalm 14.1)

"There is no God." Only fools say.

They are corrupt and go astray.

They do evil in God's sight.

Upon the earth they are a blight.

God calls from heaven to change our ways,

To live for the Lord all of our days,

To always be loving and faithfully true,

In all that we say and all that we do.

This is the day that the Lord has made,

Let us rejoice. Let our joy be displayed.

From God's hand all gifts we receive,

Thanks be to God in whom we believe.

Who Shall Dwell in God's House
(Psalm 15)

Who shall dwell in God's house?

And walk humbly in God's ways?

Those who do what is right,

Walking blamelessly always.

Those who do not slander,

Nor do evil to a friend.

Those who will help a neighbor,

Offering a hand to lend.

Those who would do good,

And strive no harm to do,

Shall always dwell in God's house,

Now and their whole life through.

Lord, You Show Me the Path of Life
(Psalm 16.11)

Lord, you show me the path of life.

In you there is joy forevermore.

You lead me beyond sin and strife.

Your mercy and grace my life restore.

By you I'm blessed beyond all measure.

I give thanks for all your mighty deeds.

In you I find pure joy and pleasure.

Abundantly you supply my needs.

I Call upon the Lord' Name
(Psalm 17.6)

I call upon the Lord's name,

For God always answers me.

I confess my sin and shame,

That forgiven I might be.

I ask for God's assistance,

To help in my time of need.

I pray with all persistence,

That God will respond indeed.

I lift to God my praises,

With Thanksgiving in my soul.

Love and joy my heart raises,

For I am again made whole.

I Will Extol You, O Lord
(Psalm 18.49)

I will extol you, O Lord,

Among all the nations,

For your deliverance,

From all of my temptations.

Lord, I offer you my prayers,

My praise to you I sing.

For all I have is a gift from you,

I thank you for everything.

When things are not going well,

I cry to you and shout.

But then I give thanks and praise,

When everything works out.

The Heavens Are Telling
(Psalm 19)

The heavens are telling the glory of God,

And so are God's many wonders on earth.

Each day reveals new creations of God,

As each long night ends a new dawn gives birth.

We celebrate all that the Lord has done,

And is doing for each one of us.

The word of the Lord enlightens each one,

To see all of God's works most precious.

Let the words which from my mouth have poured,

And the meditations of my heart each day,

Be acceptable in thy sight, O Lord,

My Rock and Redeemer, humbly I pray.

When You're in Trouble
(Psalm 20)

When you're in trouble the Lord will answer.

God Almighty will protect you.

Like how music moves a dancer,

Praying to God helps connect you.

Some will offer worldly explanations,

For how each time help comes to us.

Faith fulfills our expectations,

So, give thanks to the Lord Jesus.

The Lord will grant your heart's desire,

When you are feeling down and out.

God will raise you so much higher,

"Praise the Lord!" You'll want to shout.

Be Exalted, O Lord, in Thy Strength
(Psalm 21.13)

Be exalted, O Lord, in thy strength!

We will sing and praise thy power.

We will extol thy works at length,

During this worship hour.

You have blessed the good with grace,

The evil ones you have undone.

Thy light shines on each dark place,

Exposing sins, each and every one.

My God, My God
(Psalm 22.1)

"My God, my God,

Why hast thou forsaken me?"

We hear these words,

From the Lord at Calvary.

Upon the cross,

This old psalm Jesus quoted,

Speaking to God,

To whom he was devoted.

And though these words,

At first seem to cast a doubt,

One must read on,

To learn what the psalm's about.

The Lord Is My Shepherd
(Psalm 23)

The Lord is my shepherd,

What more do I need?

From my Lord I've heard,

That I'm loved indeed.

I am so well cared for,

In good times and bad.

I could wish for no more.

What a journey I've had!

Although we're not there yet,

A vision I see.

A banquet is set,

For all eternity.

The Earth Is the Lord's
(Psalm 24)

The earth is the Lord's and the fullness thereof,

The world and all of those who dwell therein.

For the Lord has founded it from up above,

And established it without any sin.

The perfect garden was the Lord's design,

But we have fallen from that holy place.

Eternal salvation will be yours and mine,

When we're called to come home by the Lord's grace.

The ancient gates and doors will be opened,

That the king of glory might come again.

And the Lord's Kingdom will never end,

Let all the Lord's people say, "Amen!"

O Lord, Teach Us Your Ways
(Psalm 25.4)

O Lord, teach us your ways,

Forget the sins of our younger days.

Help us now follow you,

Today and the rest of our lives through.

The examples you gave us,

Are found in the teachings of Jesus,

Who himself is the way,

We can now live through him day by day.

Today we sing your praise,

For coming to us to show us your ways.

These were shown by Jesus,

Who lived, died, and rose for each of us.

I Will Bless the Lord
(Psalm 26.12)

I will bless the Lord,

In the great congregation.

God will be adored,

By every tribe and nation.

Though few here gather,

In this local sacred space.

God's church is rather,

Everywhere and every place.

One day we will be,

The Lord's great congregation,

For all eternity,

God's ultimate creation.

The Lord Is My Light and My Salvation
(Psalm 27)

The Lord is my light and my salvation,

Whom shall I fear?

The Lord is the stronghold of my life,

And always near.

I believe I shall see God's goodness,

Throughout the land.

Wait for the Lord. Be strong and take courage.

The Lord's at hand.

There's one thing that I've asked of the Lord,

To see God's face.

And to live in God's house forever,

Blessed by God's grace.

To You, O Lord, I Call
(Psalm 28.1)

To you, O Lord, I call,

Be not deaf to me.

I pray to you my all,

And wait patiently.

All my concerns I share,

Earnestly with you.

I lift them up in prayer,

Watching what you'll do.

Thank you, Lord, for hearing,

And listening to me.

For this time of listening,

Thank you graciously.

Ascribe to the Lord Glory and Praise
(Psalm 29)

Ascribe to the Lord glory and praise.

Sing to the Lord let all voices raise.

Tell of the Lord's work of creation.

Sing hymns of praise for all the Lord's done.

When the Lord spoke all came into being,

God envisioned it all, for God is all-seeing.

And when God declared, it all happened that way.

Creation obeyed all that God did say.

Together we sing and praise the Lord's name,

God's majesty and honor we proclaim.

God sits enthroned as the Lord forever,

And we'll praise the Lord forever and ever.

Sing Praises to the Lord, You Saints
(Psalm 30)

Sing praises to the Lord, you saints.

Give thanks to the Lord's holy name.

Share prayers of thanksgiving not of complaints.

The Lord's love and mercy proclaim.

Our weeping may last for the night,

But joy does come with the morning.

The future looks hopeful and bright,

Dancing replaces our mourning.

The Lord surely eases our sorrow,

And causes our turmoil to cease.

Leading us into tomorrow,

Filled with heavenly peace.

Let Your Heart Take Courage
(Psalm 31.24)

Let your heart take courage and be strong,

All you who for the Lord wait.

The Lord will deliver you before long.

The Lord has sealed your fate.

Though turmoil and troubles come around,

And things seem at their worst,

In the Lord, miracles abound,

When we put the Lord first.

When all seems bleak and dark, seek the light.

All tunnels have an end.

At the end of the night, the dawn shines bright.

A new door is opened.

Be Glad in the Lord and Rejoice
(Psalm 32.11)

Be glad in the Lord and rejoice.

Shout for joy. Lift up your voice.

For the Lord is both forgiving,

And eternal life giving.

When God hears our confessions,

Forgiven are our transgressions.

All of our sins are washed away,

When in Jesus' name we pray.

By the Lord's hand we all are fed,

When we ask for daily bread.

The Lord gives more than we ask for.

We are blessed forevermore.

Our Soul Waits for the Lord
(Psalm 33.20)

Our soul waits for the Lord.

God is our help and shield.

Out to God our hearts are poured.

Our will to God we yield.

God always answers prayer,

As we wait patiently.

Truly God is aware,

And God's will, we will see.

The response may be "yes",

Or maybe "no" as well.

How ever God may bless,

Only time will tell.

Taste and See That the Lord Is Good
(Psalm 34.8)

Taste and see that the Lord is good!

Drink in the blessings of God's love.

For God is the giver of all things good,

Raining down from the heavens above.

Give thanks to God for all you receive,

No matter if they're bad or good.

Give thanks and praise, all who believe,

For the Lord is both great and good.

Our souls are blessed by God each day,

For we know that with God all is good.

We're blessed! Go bless others today.

Imitate God and do good.

My Tongue Shall Tell of Your Righteousness
(Psalm 35)

My tongue shall tell of your righteousness,

Singing praises all day long,

Praising in the great congregation,

In the midst of the gathered throng.

When I am overwhelmed by troubles,

When none give a hand to lend.

I rely upon God almighty,

To be my most steadfast friend.

God faithfully comes to my rescue.

The Lord is my shield and my rock.

When needed the Lord's right there with me,

Caring for the least of the flock.

How Precious Is Your Steadfast Love
(Psalm 36.7)

How precious is your steadfast love,

O Lord, of all creation!

It rains down from the heavens above,

On every land and nation.

Your love comes upon everyone,

Though only some believe it.

Bless us today to show someone,

To whom we might reveal it.

As we've been loved, so let us love,

And pass it on to others.

For all is who you are God of,

For all are sisters and brothers.

Trust in the Lord
(Psalm 37)

Trust in the Lord, and always do good,

That you may live the way that you should.

Delight in the Lord and you will be blessed.

Spend time with God and each Sabbath rest.

Wait for the Lord. Follow the Lord's way.

God will lift you, when to God you pray.

Sing to the Lord join the melody.

Shout, "Alleluia!" To God all praise be.

Believe the Lord - all that the Lord says,

Be faithful and true, that God you may bless.

Delight in the Lord and you will be blessed.

Spend time with God and each Sabbath rest.

I Confess My Iniquity
(Psalm 38.18)

I confess my iniquity,

I am sorry for my sin.

In your mercy, Lord, forgive me,

And revive my soul again.

I am lifted up by the Lord,

From the depths of where I've been.

By grace my life has been restored.

I praise the Lord once again.

Please help me, Lord, to change my ways,

So, a new life might begin.

That I may serve you all my days,

Praise God again and again!

O Lord, Hear My Prayer
(Psalm 39.12)

O Lord, hear my prayer.

To you my needs I share.

Heal my broken soul.

In you I am made whole.

When we are in pain,

Our prayers are not in vain.

As our healing starts,

God's peace will fill our hearts.

Pray for each other,

Each sister and brother.

May their struggles cease,

When we share the Lord's peace.

May All Who Seek the Lord Rejoice
(Psalm 40.16)

May all who seek the Lord rejoice.

"Great is the Lord." Shout with one voice.

As the Lord is always for us,

Sing God's praise in mighty chorus.

Worship the Lord now and always,

Come to the Lord with hymns of praise.

Confess for your sins unto the Lord,

You're forgiven. Your life is restored.

We Are Blessed

(Psalm 41)

We are blessed when we consider the poor,

When we reflect on other people's needs.

We do what we can and even do more,

Through our acts of kindness and loving deeds.

We meditate and holy contemplation,

We sing to God our praise and thanksgiving.

Blessed be the Lord of all creation,

From everlasting to everlasting.

As a Deer Longs for Flowing Streams
(Psalm 42.1)

As a deer longs for flowing streams,

My soul longs for God, so it seems.

I'm overwhelmed with guilt and grief,

My soul cries out for divine relief.

I remember those golden days,

Walking in all the Lord's ways.

I was so blessed. My life was good.

Everything was as it should.

But the joys of life then turned cold,

Unlike the wondrous days of old.

Pains and struggles now abound,

I'm lost and praying to be found.

O My Soul

(Psalm 43)

O my soul, why are you cast down?

Why in darkness do you despair?

God's great light on you has shown,

That God is always there.

God, guide me to your dwelling place,

To your holy sanctuary,

That I might behold your grace,

And for a moment tarry.

Renew my strength in that moment,

That I might be uplifted,

And once again be confident,

That by you I am gifted.

We Have Heard with Our Own Ears
(Psalm 44.1)

We have heard with our own ears,

O God, our elders have told us,

What you have done down through the years.

All praise be to the Lord Jesus.

You led Abraham and Sarah long ago,

And promised them a great future.

You showed them the land where they would go.

Their faith in you was always secure.

With Joy My Heart Overflows
(Psalm 45.1)

With joy my heart overflows.

Joyful words come from my lips.

The peace of God my soul knows.

No evil from my tongue slips.

Praising God I'll sing each day.

I'll give thanks for each blessing.

To the Lord I'll humbly pray,

Thanking God for everything.

God has been so good to me.

Every need God has addressed.

Blessings everywhere I see,

And I live a life so blessed.

God Is Our Refuge and Strength
(Psalm 46)

God is our refuge and strength,

Exalted among all of the nations.

God will go to any length,

To lead us not into temptations.

Therefore, we will never fear,

Though the whole earth should change.

For the Lord our God is here,

Strength for weakness to exchange.

God says to me, to be still,

And to know that God is God,

And that I should do God's will,

To spread Good News abroad.

All People Clap Your Hands
(Psalm 47)

All people clap your hands.

Shout to God with songs of joy!

God's blessings spread throughout the lands,

For all God's children to enjoy.

Sing praises to God, sing praises.

Sing praises with a psalm.

Our downcast spirits God raises.

We're securely held in God's palm.

Great Is the Lord
(Psalm 48)

Great is the Lord,

And greatly to be praised,

Worshipped, and adored.

By God's grace we're amazed.

We have been blessed,

And we have been forgiven.

God sent us the best,

Jesus came down from heaven.

Let us sing out,

And praise God's holy name.

Sing out and shout,

To the One who for us came.

In olden days,

He came to live among us.

We give him praise,

Give praise and thanks to Jesus.

He came to save,

Our sins to the cross he carried.

Up from the grave,

He rose up after three days buried.

Great is the Lord,

Move forevermore will be,

Worshipped and adored,

Now and for all eternity.

In Times of Trouble, I Shall Not Fear
(Psalm 49)

In times of trouble, I shall not fear,

For the Lord will see me through.

Through it all the Lord is near,

Guiding what I should do.

All who trust solely on their wealth,

And of all their riches boast,

Would give all away to restore their health,

Or whatever they prize the most.

Reflect on your life and take stock.

To follow Christ what will you give?

Like others before you, walk the walk,

That now and forever you might live.

Every Creature in the Forest
(Psalm 50)

Every creature in the forest,

All the cattle on the hill,

All birds in the air or nest,

All abide by God's will.

Unlike the other creatures,

People aren't so compliant.

They're defiant of their teachers,

Rather than obedient.

Though created in God's image,

They do not do what is right.

Wisdom does not come with age,

They do evil in God's sight.

Have Mercy on Me, O God
(Psalm 51)

Have mercy on me, O God,

According to your steadfast love.

Blot out my transgressions,

Rain down mercy from heaven above.

Wash me from my iniquity,

And cleanse me from my sin.

My sin is ever before me,

For I feel every transgression.

Create in me a clean heart,

Put a right spirit within me.

Don't cast me away but forgive,

For your spirit is most holy.

I Am Like a Green Olive Tree
(Psalm 52.8)

I am like a green olive tree,

In the midst of the House of God.

I'm blessed by all you've done for me,

Lord, I'll proclaim that your name is good.

Though turmoil is all around me,

In your presence I am at peace.

Though I am my own worst enemy,

From my chains I find release.

I am not always faithful,

I often falter day by day.

But the Lord is always grace-full,

Guiding me along the way.

God Looks Down from Heaven
(Psalm 53)

God looks down from heaven,

On all of humankind,

Seeking a glimpse of wisdom,

Wisdom of any kind.

Fools believe in their hearts,

And say, "there is no God."

They commit evil acts,

Not one of them good.

Deliver us, O God.

Restore us unto you,

Then we will be glad.

Blessed by all you do.

O God, Hear My Prayer
(Psalm 54)

O God, hear my prayer,

To my words give ear.

Petitions I share,

To me now draw near.

Troubled is my soul,

Evil is at hand.

By grace make me whole,

Able to withstand.

Always be my guide.

I'll follow your way.

With you by my side,

Your will I'll obey.

I'm Distraught by My Enemies
(Psalm 55)

I'm distraught by my enemies,

Making so much noise.

There is great shaking in my knees,

I've lost my strength and poise.

The fear of death overwhelms me.

I am always afraid,

Of all the failures that might be,

In all the plans I've made.

Almighty God I call upon,

For the Lord will save me.

By faith in God all fear is gone,

For all eternity.

In God Alone I Trust
(Psalm 56.11)

In God alone I trust,

In God, whose word I praise,

God, who is faithful and just,

And trustworthy always.

Others may be deceitful,

And try to do me harm,

But God, who's always faithful,

Will keep me safe and warm.

In every situation,

Through each trial and test,

By God's mitigation,

Always I am most blessed.

Be Merciful to Me, O God
(Psalm 57.1)

Be merciful to me, O God,

Be merciful to me.

For in you my soul takes refuge,

Saved by grace I'll always be.

Every day there are temptations,

Difficulties galore.

Yet I am blessed, for by your grace,

I'm saved forevermore.

I will celebrate your mercy,

Which you so freely give.

Forever I will praise your name,

And in your presence live.

The Righteous Will Rejoice
(Psalm 58.10)

The righteous will rejoice,

And praise the Lord above.

They will lift up their voice,

And give to God their love.

But what of those who sin?

The Lord will pass judgment.

In the end God will win,

God will be triumphant.

Repent of every sin,

That from God separates.

Let a new life begin,

Behold the golden gates.

O God, You Are My Fortress
(Psalm 59.17)

O God, you are my fortress.

I sing praises to you.

A refuge in my distress,

To you all praise is due.

When I'm overwhelmed by things,

You are Lord overall.

And so, my spirit sings,

To you these things are small.

When I struggle at length,

And problems are too great,

I rely on your strength,

Your love overcomes hate.

Give Victory and Answer Us
(Psalm 60.5)

Give victory and answer us,

That we may be rescued.

For you have sent the Lord Jesus.

With the Lord all is good.

As your people we celebrate,

All things that you have done.

Your gracious love overcame hate,

Over sin grace has won.

To you we give our thanks and praise,

For all you've done before.

We will rejoice all of our days,

Now and forevermore.

O God, Hear My Cry
(Psalm 61.1)

O God, hear my cry.

Listen to my prayer.

On you I rely,

My petitions I share.

Times are difficult,

Each and every day.

A personal assault,

Seems to come my way.

I am lost without you,

Frail and weak alone.

All things with you I can do,

With you all can be done.

Truly in God My Soul Finds Rest
(Psalm 62.1)

Truly in God my soul finds rest.

My salvation comes from the Lord.

I am each day by God blessed.

My faith is renewed and restored.

To the Lord I will sing my praise,

And rejoice for all the Lord's done.

To the Lord my prayers I will raise.

By God the victory is won.

My eternal life I entrust,

To the Lord who came to save.

Ashes to ashes and dust to dust,

But eternal life I'll have.

God, My Soul Thirsts for You
(Psalm 63)

God, my soul thirsts for you,

As in a dry and thirsty land,

Where no water is near at hand.

It is you that I pursue.

I've seen you in the sanctuary,

My lips praise you all day long.

I tell your story with my song.

I've seen your power and glory.

I proclaim your grace day and night.

You will protect me with your wings.

For my salvation my heart sings.

With you, Lord, all will be alright.

Let the Righteous Rejoice
(Psalm 64.10)

Let the righteous rejoice in the Lord,

When through God's grace their lives are restored.

Let all whose hearts are in the right place,

Give praise to the Lord for the Lord's grace.

But those who are wandering or are lost,

Return to the Lord at any cost,

To turn from their ways of wrong and sin,

To open their hearts and let Jesus in.

Let all the doubters come to believe,

That through Jesus new life they'll receive.

May they be moved from darkness to light,

And by the Lord may they do what is right.

Holy God of Zion
(Psalm 65.1)

Holy God of Zion,

To you even silence is praise.

When promises are kept,

Your will is done somehow some ways.

For you who hears our thoughts,

And knows what is in every heart,

Receive our prayers and thoughts and deeds,

As we each humbly do our part.

In silence we are blessed,

When we come into your presence.

We are touched in our very souls,

By your holy eminence.

Shout Joyfully to God, All the Earth
(Psalm 66.1)

Shout joyfully to God, of the earth.

Shout joyfully for all you're worth.

Sing praises to the glory of God's name.

Sing praises let the whole world do the same.

For all that the Lord has done for us,

Especially sending us Jesus,

Who taught his disciples how to live,

And died salvation to us give.

Give thanks for all that the Lord has done.

Through Jesus the victory is won.

Alleluia! Praise the Lord above!

Who first loved us and calls us to love.

Let God Bless Us and Grant Us Grace
(Psalm 67)

Let God bless us and grant us grace,

Shining upon each blessed face.

In order that God's way be known,

And we choose God's way for our own.

God, let all the people thank you,

For all you have done and will do.

Let all the people celebrate,

Let all the people on you wait.

Let God continue to bless us,

Through the teachings of Jesus.

In God Almighty we believe,

And God's mercy we receive.

Join the Great Procession
(Psalm 68)

Join the great procession,

Coming to the Lord,

Offer your confession,

Let your soul be restored.

The acolytes with fire,

And singers lead the band,

The preachers who inspire,

With liturgists at hand.

Into the sanctuary,

They come down the aisle.

It's extraordinary,

All in single file.

Save Me, God
(Psalm 69)

Save me, God,

For enemies persecute me.

Help me, God,

That blessed forever I shall be.

Save me, God,

For I had hoped for sympathy.

Help me, God,

And friends, I could not find any.

Save me, God,

You know I wept while I fasted.

Help me, God,

For that too I was insulted.

Let All Who Seek the Lord Rejoice
(Psalm 70.4)

Let all who seek the Lord rejoice,

Let them say, "God is great!"

God, give them strength in heart and voice,

As they upon you wait.

Let all who seek the Lord today,

Say, "God is Lord of all!"

Let all then humbly to God pray,

And upon God's name call.

Let all who seek the Lord be found,

Let them say, "God is love!"

May they spread God's love all around,

Passed down from God above.

As for Me, I Will Hope Always
(Psalm 71)

As for me, I will hope always,

To God I will sing praise.

I will tell of God's righteous deeds,

That supply all our needs.

The Lord Almighty blesses us,

Through the words of Jesus.

And by his resurrection we,

Will live eternally.

Join in with me and sing this song,

Praise the Lord all day long.

No matter what the day might bring,

Praise to God we will sing.

Lord, Let There Be Abundant Grain
(Psalm 72)

Lord, let there be abundant grain.

In the pastures let it wave.

Bless the earth with abundant rain,

By your hand, our lives you save.

Lord, let there be all that we need.

For this we most humbly pray.

For each plant with lifegiving seed,

We give thanks to you today.

Lord, let fruits flourish in season,

Each harvest in abundance.

We praise your name for this reason,

Your glorious providence.

God Is Good to Israel
(Psalm 73)

God is good to Israel,

To those who have pure hearts.

But me? My feet have stumbled.

I move with fits and starts.

I have envied the arrogant.

The wicked are well off.

They aren't weighed down like others.

Even at God they scoff.

But me? It is good for me,

To be near the Lord God.

I will speak of God's good works.

For each I will applaud.

God, the Day Belongs to You
(Psalm 74.16)

God, the day belongs to you,

And also, the nighttime too.

You made both the moon and sun.

Back when creation was begun.

You set all earth's boundaries.

Creating all as you please.

Each season got its limit.

That all might live within it.

What wondrous works God has done,

Everything under the sun.

Come join together. Sing God's praise,

And worship the Lord always.

We Give Thanks to You, God
(Psalm 75.1)

We give thanks to you, God, we give thanks.

Your marvelous deeds are declared.

We gather in worship and sing your praise.

Our prayers and petitions are shared.

In worship we read your holy word.

We remember your mighty deeds.

We give thanks for your mercy and love,

And how your grace meets all our needs.

When Promising the Lord, Take Care
(Psalm 76.11)

When promising the Lord, take care,

That you'll fulfill it fully.

For you shall be judged then and there,

If it's been done faithfully.

It is not just what we believe,

For it matters what we do.

It is not just what we conceive,

But also, our follow through.

By others may your faith be known,

Through your actions and your prayers.

And may your faithfulness be shown,

In the Lord of Life who cares.

We Will Remember the Lord's Deeds
(Psalm 77.11)

We will remember the Lord's deeds,

Wondrous acts from times past.

Making a path through the Sea of Reeds,

A way to freedom at last.

In the wilderness, nothing to eat,

No water was to be found.

Manna and quail were at our feet,

Water from a rock on the ground.

When we've wandered, you've been there,

Helping us to find the way.

We are blessed by your loving care.

We rejoice and give thanks today.

Tell the Next Generation
(Psalm 78.4)

Tell the next generation,

The wondrous work that God has done.

Tell it to every nation,

To all people under the sun.

Down throughout our history,

God has faithfully been with us,

Sometimes veiled in mystery,

But then God sent us Jesus.

Jesus revealed God's glory,

Through miracles and signs.

Jesus taught us God's story,

Through lost sheep and fruitful vines.

We Are God's People After All
(Psalm 79.13)

We are God's people after all,

Sheep of the Lord's pasture.

For God is great and we are small,

With God we will endure.

Tough times don't last, tough people do,

Or so the saying goes.

Our faith in God will see us through,

To joy beyond our woes.

Do not give up. Hold onto God.

You're held in the Lord's hands.

By the Lord's grace go out and spread,

God's peace throughout the lands.

Restore Us, Lord God
(Psalm 80.19)

Restore us, Lord God.

Make your face shine.

That we can be saved,

By your hand divine.

We've sinned against you.

We've fallen away,

By the things that we do,

And the words that we say.

From heaven above,

By your mercy and grace,

You show us your love,

For the whole human race.

God Feeds Us the Finest Wheat
(Psalm 81.16)

God feeds us the finest wheat.

Satisfies us with honey sweet.

The fruit of the vine fills our cup.

With thanks to God, we lift it up.

For all our needs God does provide.

For all of our sins, Christ has died.

And as in faith he rose again,

The gate to heaven is now open.

There he sits upon his throne,

And calls to him all of his own,

That we might from our labors rest,

For we will be forever blessed.

Rise Up God
(Psalm 82.8)

Rise up God! Judge the earth.

You hold the world in your possession.

You grant to us your divine worth.

Hear our humble confession.

We have failed you so many ways,

By the things that we have done.

We have sinned both nights and days,

Since creation was begun.

Please, Lord, set us straight today.

Help us to follow you,

That we might walk your holy way,

And do all we can do.

God, Do Not Be Silent
(Psalm 83.1)

God, do not be silent.

Don't be quiet or still.

Speak and give us guidance,

That we might do your will.

Give us your instruction,

That we might truly be,

Your faithful disciples,

For all eternity.

Share with us your wisdom.

Fill us with your Good News.

Give to us your power,

To change don'ts into dos.

Better Is a Single Day
(Psalm 84.10)

Better is a single day,

In your company,

Then a thousand days,

Spent elsewhere any.

It's a joy to be with you,

Following your way.

Your love sees us through.

We rejoice today.

You give to us our rest,

As we gather here.

We are in you blessed,

When we feel you near.

Faithful Love and Truth Have Met
(Psalm 85)

Faithful love and truth have met.

Righteousness and peace have kissed.

The Lord's Mercy has paid the debt.

Our sins have been erased.

Yes, the Lord gives what is good,

And the Lord's land yields its produce.

The Lord gives to us our food.

The Lord gives all for our use.

Celebrate and praise the Lord,

For the Lord's generosity.

May the Lord's name be adored,

Now and for all eternity.

Lord, Listen Closely to Me
(Psalm 86.1)

Lord, listen closely to me,

For I am poor and in need.

I pray to you on bended knee,

For your mercy, I plead.

Lord, give to me an answer.

Reveal to me your sign.

Now, my faith reassure,

By your grace divine.

Moving forward guide me,

Along your sacred way,

That I might always be,

Faithful day by day.

People Praise God as They Sing
(Psalm 87.7)

People praise God as they sing,

"The source of my life is you!"

And to God they pray and bring,

Themselves as an offering that's due.

For all we have and all we are,

Are God's gifts given to us.

For our sins we do not despair,

Salvation comes through Jesus.

Our troubled souls. Jesus does lift,

Setting us on the way.

By his everlasting gift,

We receive new life each day.

Lord, I Cry Out to You
(Psalm 88.13)

Lord, I cry out to you,

First thing in the morning.

To you, my prayer gets through.

As the day is dawning.

Lord, I call out to you,

In the midst of the day,

Asking what I should do.

For your wisdom, I pray.

Lord, I pray to you,

When I lay down at night.

For all that we've been through,

With you all is alright.

We Will Sing of God's Love Forever
(Psalm 89.1)

We will sing of God's love forever,

Down through the generations.

Praising God over and over,

Here and throughout the nations.

We will praise God's mighty deeds,

Miracles new and old.

We will plant the fruitful seeds,

As each story is retold.

We will proclaim God's Good News,

To those who've not yet heard.

Offering our enlightened views,

Upon God's holy word.

Lord, Our Help Has Come from You
(Psalm 90)

Lord, our help has come from you,

Each day, our whole lives through,

Down through the generations,

And throughout the nations.

You return people to dust,

Like yesterday when past,

Like grass fresh in the morning,

Yet dried up by the evening.

At best, we may live to seventy,

If we're strong, maybe eighty.

Teach us to number our days,

That we may know your wise ways.

All Who Love God Will Be Delivered
(Psalm 91.14)

All who love God will be delivered,

All who call upon God's name.

God will answer everyone,

Giving mercy to the same.

Whenever we're in trouble,

The Lord will see us through.

Whenever we can't find the way,

God comes to our rescue.

God will give to us long life,

A most prosperous one.

When we look back where we've been,

We'll see all God has done.

Lord, by Your Works You've Made Me Glad
(Psalm 92.4)

Lord, by all your works, you've made me glad.

By all you've done, I sing for joy.

You are my rock when things go bad.

You have given me life to enjoy.

I give thanks for all you've created.

You have made the most wondrous things.

To you I am ingratiated.

For all you've done, my heart sings.

I come to worship to sing your praises,

For everything you've done for me.

I will follow you all my days,

Now and for all eternity.

The Lord Is Robed in Majesty
(Psalm 93)

The Lord is robed in majesty.

The Lord Almighty reigns.

The Lord on high is mighty,

Above the hills and plains.

Mightier than the waves on the sea,

Mightier than the flood waters,

The Lord is high and mighty.

Rejoice you sons and daughters.

The Lord rules with mercy.

The Lord's decrees are sure.

The Lord on high is mighty.

The Lord reigns forevermore.

The Lord Has Become My Stronghold
(Psalm 94.22)

The Lord has become my stronghold.

My God is the rock of my refuge.

In praise of the Lord, I become bold.

In a world of small problems, God's huge.

The Lord will be my protector,

Whenever I find I'm in need.

The Lord is thus the main character.

The Lord will be there for me indeed.

Come, Let's Worship and Bow Down
(Psalm 95)

Come, let's worship and bow down,

Before the Lord, our maker, kneel.

The Lord's majesty is renown.

The Lord's love in our hearts we feel.

Don't harden your hearts again,

Like you did at Meribah.

In disbelief, way back when,

In the desert of Massah.

Learn lessons on faith's journey,

Of what all the Lord can do.

For struggles always will be,

Times for our faith to renew.

Let Heaven Celebrate
(Psalm 96.11)

Let heaven celebrate.

Let the earth rejoice.

Let the sea lie prostrate.

Or roar with great noise.

Let all the countryside,

Also celebrate,

And let the forest wide,

Shout, "The Lord is great!"

Let all creation show,

The Lord's majesty.

That the whole world might know,

God is almighty.

The Lord Rules
(Psalm 97.1)

The Lord rules. Let the earth rejoice!

Let all the people celebrate.

Together sing with one voice.

Let all shout, "the Lord is great!"

Before Creation was begun,

The Spirit moved over the sea.

We celebrate the Lord is one.

Three in one - the Trinity.

And then, just when the time was right,

All was made by the spoken Word.

Nothing happened in God's sight,

Till that empowering Word was heard.

Sing to the Lord a New Song
(Psalm 98.1)

Sing to the Lord a new song,

For the Lord has done wondrous things.

With praises sing all day long,

For each blessing the Lord brings.

Celebrate all God has done,

And is still doing today.

So, before this day is done,

With thanksgiving, let us pray.

To the Lord, lift up your praise.

Let your heartfelt praises ring.

Praise the Lord for all of your days.

To the Lord, a new song sing.

Magnify the Lord Our God
(Psalm 99.9)

Magnify the Lord our God!

Because the Lord our God is holy.

Clap your hands and applaud.

Worship the Lord our God solely.

The Lord our God is almighty,

Worthy of our thanks and praise.

Now and for all eternity,

Worship the Lord our God always.

The Lord our God in heaven reigns.

Even before creation.

And now through us, the Lord proclaims,

Good News to every nation.

Because the Lord Is Good
(Psalm 100.5)

Because the Lord is good,

The Lord's love lasts forever,

Just as it always should,

Faithful forever and ever.

Because the Lord is good,

God's love remains a given.

Whenever we repent to God,

Our sins shall be forgiven.

Because the Lord is good,

We always will be blessed.

All will be well as it should,

When to God, we have confessed.

Let Me Sing of Love and Justice
(Psalm 101.1)

Let me sing of love and justice,

To the Lord sing praises.

Let me sing of the love of Jesus,

Revealed in scripture phrases.

The poor and sick were lifted up,

And the lost sheep were found.

Christ is revealed in bread and cup.

In him I'm safe and sound.

Though all have sinned and fallen short,

Sinners are forgiven.

Through Christ people will find comfort,

Welcomed into heaven.

Lord, Hear My Humble Prayer
(Psalm 102.1)

Lord, here, my humble prayer.

Let my cry reach you.

My soul to you I bare,

That you will see me through.

I turn to you alone.

No one else is there.

You hear my deepest groan,

In my dark despair.

I don't know just when,

You will respond to me.

I will be restored then,

For all eternity.

Let My Soul Bless the Lord
(Psalm 103.1)

Let my soul bless the Lord,

Bless God's holy name.

Let my soul bless the Lord,

Let's all do the same.

Let my soul bless the Lord,

For all God has done.

Let my soul bless the Lord.

Praise the holy One.

Let my soul bless the Lord,

In whom, my life begins.

Let my soul bless the Lord,

Who forgives all my sins.

I Will Sing to the Lord
(Psalm 104.33)

I will sing to the Lord,

For as long as I live.

I will sing praises to God,

While I am still alive.

I will lift up my prayer,

And to God bare my soul.

God, with mercy and care,

Will again make me whole.

I will follow the Lord,

And love as God loves me.

The Lord will be adored,

For all eternity.

Give Thanks to the Lord
(Psalm 105.1)

Give thanks to the Lord.

Make the Lord's deeds known to all.

Sing praises to the Lord.

For miracles great and small.

Give thanks to the Lord,

For the things done in ancient days.

Sing praises to the Lord,

For being with us always.

Give thanks to the Lord,

Who led Israel by the hand.

Sing praises to the Lord,

Who led them to the promised land.

Give Thanks for the Lord Is Good
(Psalm 106.1)

Give thanks, for the Lord is good.

God's love endures forever.

So let it be understood,

God won't forsake us ever.

As far as east is from west,

God removes all of our sins.

By the love of God we're blessed,

As new life in Christ begins.

Let's praise the Lord forever.

Let us always sing God's praise.

From Christ's love none can sever.

We will worship God always.

Give Thanks to the Lord When You Pray
(Psalm 107)

"Give thanks to the Lord when you pray,

For the Lord's love lasts forever."

That's what those redeemed by the Lord say.

The Lord abandons them never.

Into the desert some did roam,

And there, they could not find their way.

They could not find their way home.

There their lives were slipping away.

God heard their cry and their distress.

They were delivered from their fate.

God answered them, and them did bless.

Back to safety, God led them straight.

Some had gone out on the high seas,

Where storms arose with mighty waves.

In fear, they fell down on their knees.

God calmed the storm, for the Lord saves.

Lord, I'll Give Thanks

(Psalm 108.3)

Lord, I'll give thanks to you,

Among all the nations,

And I'll make music too,

With great celebrations.

For all you've done, I'll sing,

And give you all the praise.

To you offerings I'll bring,

And worship you always.

With joy praises are poured,

Upon your holy name.

You're worshipped and adored,

As our faith we proclaim.

We celebrate your grace,

For you have set us free;

In heaven made us space,

For all eternity.

I Will Give to the Lord

(Psalm 109.30)

I will give to the Lord thanks,

Among a great crowd.

For above all the Lord ranks,

I'll praise God aloud.

In every situation,

Each and every day,

There's cause for celebration.

Praise God anyway.

Even in the worst of days,

It could still be worse.

Take time to give God praise,

Sing to God this verse.

The Lord will restore you.

Believe the holy text.

The Lord will see you through,

In this world or the next.

God Brings the Nations to Justice

(Psalm 110.6)

God brings the nations to justice.

The way of the Lord is true.

The way of the Lord is righteous.

God is making all things new.

In Jesus, God revealed the Way,

That all might live in peace.

When people do what God does say,

Then, finally, wars will cease.

We live in imperfection,

Until the perfect comes.

God will rule over each nation,

When the whole world succumbs.

Jesus, come fulfill your story,

For us, Eden restore.

Lead us, Jesus, onto glory,

And reign forevermore.

The Works of the Lord Are Magnificent

(Psalm 111)

The works of the Lord are magnificent.

They are treasured, for they are heaven sent.

God's deeds are majestic and glorious.

We give thanks for all that God does for us.

God is full of compassion and mercy.

The Lord gives food to all who are hungry.

The Lord's handiwork is honest and just.

God's commandments are worthy of trust.

God's rules are forever established,

Awaiting for all to be accomplished.

From the fear of the Lord all wisdom came.

Holy and awesome is God's precious name.

Those Who Honor the Lord Are Blessed

(Psalm 112)

Those who honor the Lord are blessed.

Their righteousness stands forever.

They give to God their very best.

God blesses each endeavor.

The faithful rise to meet the day,

Asking God what they might do.

By doing what they hear God say,

They bless God the whole day through.

May we be people of such faith,

As we serve our Lord always.

That we might faithfully live with,

The hope that we'll see God's face.

Let the Lord's Name Be Blessed

(Psalm 113)

Let the Lord's name be blessed,

From now until forever,

And your faith be professed,

Forever and ever.

Let the Lord's name be praised,

From sunrise to sunrise,

And all voices be raised,

To God above the skies.

Let the Lord's name be shared,

With those who feel left out,

And may their voices be spared,

When the Lord's name they shout.

When Israel Came out of Egypt

(Psalm 114)

When Israel came out of Egypt,

By God they were equipped.

Judah was God's sanctuary.

Israel was God's territory.

The sea parted and retreated,

At the Jordan, it was repeated.

Mountains leapt away like rams.

Hills leapt away like lambs.

Before the Lord, the earth trembled.

Before the Lord, all was humbled.

A pool of water came from a stone.

All came from God and God alone.

Idols Are Just Things

(Psalm 115)

Idols are just things,

Made by human hands.

Their mouth never sings,

Nor shout out commands.

Their eyes cannot see,

Nor can their ears hear.

Their hands cannot be,

Used to draw things near.

Their feet cannot walk.

Their noses can't smell.

Their mouths cannot talk.

They've nothing to tell.

But our God is real.

We will bless the Lord.

Let us now reveal,

That God is adored.

God Is Merciful and Righteous

(Psalm 116.5)

God is merciful and righteous.

Our God is compassionate.

The Lord is ever more gracious,

When we are most obstinate.

With joy, let us now celebrate,

All that the Lord's done for us.

We give thanks, for the Lord is great.

Give glory to Christ Jesus.

Sins are completely forgiven,

When we ask the Lord for grace,

And we catch a glimpse of heaven,

Glow in each penitent face.

Praise the Lord, All You Nations

(Psalm 117)

God's faithful love for us is strong.

God's faithfulness lasts forever.

We glorify God with our song.

Our gratitude shall cease never.

Praise the Lord, all you nations.

Praise God, all generations.

O God, we come to worship you,

With one accord, our voice we raise.

Giving thanks for all that you do,

As we sing, hear our heartfelt praise.

Praise the Lord, all you nations.

Praise God, all generations.

Give Thanks to the Lord

(Psalm 118)

Give thanks to the Lord, for God is good.

The Lord's faithful love lasts forever.

God will save us, for only God could.

Nothing can harm us whatsoever.

The stone rejected by the builders,

Has become the very cornerstone.

This belief, to some, bewilders.

Salvation comes from Christ alone.

Give thanks to the Lord, for God is good.

The Lord's faithful love lasts forever.

God will save us, for only God could.

Nothing can harm us whatsoever.

Lord, Let Your Salvation Come to Me

(Psalm 119.41)

Lord, let your salvation come to me,

According to your promise.

May your promises always be,

True, like arrows that do not miss.

I celebrate your holy word,

And ponder all you've said.

From childhood your message I have heard.

Your word rules my heart and head.

I repent of how I have behaved,

For I have broken your law.

But by your mercy, I have been saved.

You forgive my every flaw.

I Cried out to God

(Psalm 120)

I cried out to God when I was distressed,

And there in my prayer, the Lord answered me.

When God answered me, my soul was so blessed,

That my prayer was heard by God Almighty.

I've lived far too long with haters of peace.

I am for peace, but they are for war.

I am praying for all wars to cease,

That people might come to learn war no more.

Wherever you are, whatever is wrong,

God's not far away. God is always there.

God is there with you, for there you belong.

All will be alright. You are in God's care.

I Raise My Eyes to the Hills

(Psalm 121)

I raise my eyes to the hills.

Where will salvation come from?

All promises God fulfills.

From God all our blessings come.

May God each day be adored,

And may our faith never fade.

Protection is from the Lord,

Beside you just like a shade.

The sun won't strike you by day,

Nor will the moon in the night.

As long as we're on the way,

With God, all shall be right.

Peace Be with Jerusalem

(Psalm 122)

Peace be with Jerusalem,

For the House of God's sake.

So that for all of them,

Let us lasting peace make.

Pray that there is true peace.

Let those that love God rest.

That hostilities cease,

And all people be blessed.

Give thanks to the Lord's name,

Who gives mercy and grace.

To the world we proclaim,

This is God's holy place.

O Lord, Have Mercy upon Us

(Psalm 123)

O Lord, have mercy upon us,

For we have had more than enough.

We cry out to you, Jesus,

Save us from all of this stuff.

We come before you today,

Longing for your presence.

We come to hear what you say,

Give us your sustenance.

Help us share what we've heard,

And what we've come to know.

We will proclaim your word,

Everywhere that we go.

If the Lord Hadn't Been for Us

(Psalm 124.1)

If the Lord hadn't been for us,

Let God's holy people now say,

If the Lord hadn't been for us,

We never would have found the way.

If the Lord hadn't been for us,

When enemies threatened,

If the Lord hadn't been for us,

None would have come to defend.

If the Lord hadn't been for us,

We would have drowned in the sea,

If the Lord hadn't been for us,

And we no longer would be.

If the Lord hadn't been for us,

Let God's holy people now say,

If the Lord hadn't been for us,

We would not be here today.

As the Mountains Surround Jerusalem

(Psalm 125.2)

As the mountains surround Jerusalem,

So, the Lord surrounds all of the people.

Peace be on the people, upon all of them.

Let peace ring out from the bells in the steeple.

Give thanks to God who rules high above us,

And guides us all to follow faithfully.

Give thanks to God who sent us Christ Jesus,

Who calls us all to follow him fully.

Our Tongues Were Filled with Joyful Shouts

(Psalm 126.2)

Our tongues were filled with joyful shouts.

It was said among the nations,

"God always knows their whereabouts,

And blesses their congregations."

We celebrate all God has done,

Come before God and let us pray.

We are blessed each and every one.

We are blessed each and every day.

Come to God with your offering.

Bring to God heartfelt words of praise.

And to the Lord let us now sing,

Forever and ever always.

Unless It Is the Lord

(Psalm 127)

Unless it is the Lord who builds the house,

The workers all waste time on construction,

Not knowing all the whats, wheres, whys, and hows,

For it will fall in utter destruction.

Children are a gift from a loving Lord,

There is no doubt about it. We are blessed.

The fruit of the womb is a divine reward,

And there is no doubt, children are the best.

Everyone Who Walks in God's Ways

(Psalm 128)

Everyone who walks in God's ways,

Is truly happy always.

You will enjoy all that you do,

And all things will go well for you.

You'll be blessed in so many ways,

A long life filled with good days.

God will provide all of the best,

Among all, you will be blessed.

Children's children will be your gift,

They will all your days uplift.

That's how it is for everyone,

God blesses from Mount Zion.

From My Youth I Have Been Attacked

(Psalm 129)

From my youth I have been attacked,

But no one has defeated me.

From the Lord nothing have I lacked.

The Lord has blessed me faithfully.

When threats and dangers start to grow,

And others gather to speak maliciously,

I give thanks to the God I know,

Praying that the Lord will save me.

I pray that someday there will come,

A time when the world with peace is filled,

And spread to all, not just to some.

Then all will be as God has willed.

To God I Cry Out

(Psalm 130)

From the depths, to God I cry out,

My Lord, listen to my plea.

You can help me. I have no doubt.

Hear my request for mercy.

My whole being waits for the Lord,

Like the night watch waits for dawn.

Upon the Lord my heart's been poured.

God is the one I wait upon.

When all is bad and even worse,

It's not always as it seems.

Remember this powerful verse,

God through Christ all sin redeems.

My Eyes Are Never Raised Too High

(Psalm 131)

My eyes are never raised too high.

I've calmed and quieted my soul.

Most things I'm never bothered by,

Or they would surely take their toll.

Especially when times are stressed,

To God I pray for perfect peace.

Thanks be to God for I am blessed,

When all to God I release.

God hear me when I call to you,

When I'm having one of those days.

Guide me again what I should do,

That turmoil can be turned to praise.

David Vowed unto You, Lord

(Psalm 132.1)

David vowed unto you, Lord,

That he'd do what thou wilt.

All materials he had stored,

That your temple would be built.

David vowed to never rest,

Till he built a place for you,

A place where you would be blessed,

While you blessed the people too.

Yet you affirmed for the king,

Children would sit on his throne,

For you can do anything.

You are God and God alone.

Look How Pleasing and How Good

(Psalm 133)

Look how pleasing and how good,

When families can live as one,

Like one caring neighborhood,

When everything's said and done.

It is like expensive oil,

Poured on the head and beard,

On priests who to God were loyal,

Who told the people God's word.

Like Mount Hermon's holy dew,

Into the valleys flowing,

Bringing things alive, anew,

Where the Spirit is blowing.

All You Who Serve the Lord

(Psalm 134.1)

All you who serve the Lord,

Bless the Lord right now!

On you God's love is poured,

As you fulfill your vow.

Chorus:

As you leave this place,

Go on out to share.

Look into each face,

Share God everywhere.

Enter God's house in prayer.

Lift up your hands in praise,

Serve God right then and there.

Serve God all of your days,

Chorus:

Lord, Your Name is Forever

(Psalm 135.13)

Lord, your name is forever!

Lord, your fame extends far out,

Both here and wherever,

Your people are about.

We celebrate on hilltops,

And in valleys down below,

Wherever we make stops,

Wherever else we go.

No matter where we wander,

No matter where we roam,

You are over yonder,

And right here at home.

God's Faithful Love Lasts Forever

(Psalm 136)

Give thanks to the Lord of us all.

No matter what, God is for us.

Give thanks both the tall and the small.

Sing praise in mighty chorus.

God's faithful love lasts forever!

God made the sun to rule the day,

And the moon and stars to rule the night.

God put the heavens on display.

Look up and see the Lord's delight.

God's faithful love lasts forever!

Give thanks to God who split the sea.

Give thanks to God who brought us out.

Give thanks to God who set us free.

Give thanks and give a shout.

God's faithful love lasts forever!

How Can We Sing Our Faithful Songs

(Psalm 137)

How can we sing our faithful songs,

In the midst of all of life's wrongs?

Israel cried in Babylon.

How could they possibly go on?

They hung their lyres up in the trees,

As they fell down upon their knees.

How could they possibly sing there,

In that land so full of despair?

All they could sing would be laments,

Filled with the worst hateful comments,

Wishing destruction for their foes,

With file words their hatred shows.

I Give Thanks with All My Heart

(Psalm 138.1)

I give thanks with all my heart,

To the Lord I sing my praise.

God's been with me since the start,

From the youngest of my days.

I bow down and lift God's name,

When I come to God in prayer.

I'm never then quite the same,

Whenever I leave from there.

God touches my very soul.

God forgives and loves me so.

Broken pieces are made whole.

Set free, now I'm free to go.

Lord, You Have Examined Me

(Psalm 139)

Lord, you have examined me.

You know when I sit or stand.

You know me intimately,

What all I think and have planned.

There is nowhere I can go.

I can't get away from you.

Wherever I am, I know,

That you can find me there too.

Lord, you have created me.

You fashioned me together.

I was made marvelously,

Unique and like no other.

From Evil People Rescue Me

(Psalm 140.1)

From evil people, rescue me.

Lord, guard me from their violence.

When I'm closed in, please set me free.

May my soul find sacred silence.

At times I feel I can't go on.

Obstacles block and stop my way.

When my strength is completely gone,

To you I desperately pray.

Right then I know no matter what,

When things seem to be at their worst,

I try to fix things myself but,

I should have come to you, Lord, first.

O Lord, I Cry out to You

(Psalm 141.1)

O Lord, I cry out to you.

Listen to the sound of my voice.

Guide me in what I should do,

And I will greatly rejoice.

Strengthen me for the journey,

At times the climb will be steep.

At times it will be easy,

There I will find time to sleep.

Guide me onto your right path,

For I have wandered away.

Save me from your holy wrath,

Guide me upon the right way.

I Cry Out for Help

(Psalm 142.1)

I cry out for help with my needs.

I beg out loud for mercy.

Unto God my weary soul pleads.

O Lord, please deliver me.

When I find myself in the pits,

And life is overwhelming.

And I feel like calling it quits,

God's word to me is calming.

Though this seems bad, Lord, we faced worse,

And you've always helped me through.

Speak to me through a scripture verse.

Reveal to me what to do.

As you have guided in the past,

Once again, guide me today.

Strengthen my faith now to hold fast,

To you, O Lord, this I pray.

O Lord, Listen to My Prayer

(Psalm 143.1)

O Lord, listen to my prayer,

Because of your faithfulness.

With you my desires I share,

Because of your righteousness.

Whenever I am in need,

Because of your faithfulness.

To you, O Lord, do I plead,

Because of your righteousness.

Petitions to you I bring,

Because of your faithfulness.

And praises to you I sing,

Because of your righteousness.

Blessed Be the Lord

(Psalm 144)

Blessed be the Lord, my rock and fortress,

My deliverer, and my stronghold.

By the Lord my soul is always most blessed.

With God's assurance I can be bold.

Lord, who are humans that you regard us?

Our days are much like a passing shadow.

To forgive our sins you sent us Jesus,

That your love and mercy we all might know.

May all our livestock bear healthy offspring.

May our barns be filled with produce and grain.

May we lift to you prayers of thanksgiving.

May we share our faith again and again.

The Lord Is Great

(Psalm 145)

The Lord is great and so worthy of praise.

God's greatness cannot be comprehended.

Each generation will praise you always.

Your mighty acts shall be never ended.

God is merciful and compassionate,

Very patient and full of faithful love.

The Lord's mercy and grace are infinite.

Love is what all God has made, is made of.

The Lord's praise, my mouth will proclaim.

God is close to everyone who calls out.

Every living thing will bless God's name.

The Lord will bless us without a doubt.

Praise the Lord

(Psalm 146)

Praise the Lord!

Let my whole being praise the Lord,

Praise God as long as I live.

God's the one to be adored,

To whom all praises I give.

Praise the Lord!

Don't trust human beings,

When they die their plans are gone.

Praise God with your thanksgivings,

For God's plans go on and on.

Praise the Lord!

God who made heaven and earth,

God is faithful forever.

God declared our sacred worth,

And abandons us never.

Praise the Lord!

The Lord who loves the righteous,

And helps orphans and widows,

Looks out for each one of us,

Upon us mercy bestows.

Praise the Lord!

God Heals the Broken Hearted

(Psalm 147)

God heals the broken hearted.

Our Lord is great and strong.

God fulfills what was started.

Let us praise God with our song.

God's knowledge cannot be grasped.

Sing to the Lord God with praise.

God has led us in the past,

Leads us now, and will always.

As the seasons come and go,

We proclaim God's holy name.

Though the tides both ebb and flow,

The Lord God remains the same.

Praise the Lord from Heaven

(Psalm 148)

Praise the Lord from heaven!

Praise God, angels on high,

Also, the sun and moon,

And all up in the sky.

Praise the Lord from the earth,

And in the oceans deep!

Each creature from its birth,

Until it's final sleep.

Let all praise the Lord's name,

Including rocks and hills.

Let all life do the same,

For this is what God wills.

Sing to the Lord a New Song

(Psalm 149.1)

Sing to the Lord a new song.

Sing God's praise with the faithful.

Sing to the Lord all day long.

For all God does we're grateful.

To the Lord offer glory.

To the Lord offer your praise.

Retell again God's story.

And sing to the Lord always.

Celebrate all God has done.

With joyful hearts let us sing.

Praise the Lord the three in one,

And give thanks for everything.

Praise God in the Sanctuary

(Psalm 150)

Praise God in the sanctuary.

Praise God in the dome and sky.

Praise God in the estuary,

In all places low and high.

Praise God in the wind and the fire.

Praise God with the ram's horn sound.

Praise God with the lute and the lyre.

Let the people's praise resound.

Praise God with loud clashing symbols.

Praise God with the pipe and strings.

In harmony the mountain rumbles,

When to God the whole world sings.

Reverend Jeff Childs has devoted more than 40 years to serving God through ordained ministry in the United Methodist Church. Throughout his pastoral career, he has written sermons, Bible studies, and articles that reflect his deep faith and commitment to the church. Beyond the pulpit, he has engaged in mission work across the United States and Central America—helping to build, repair, and worship with communities impacted by natural disasters and hardship. These experiences have deeply shaped his ministry and enriched his writing with wisdom and compassion.

Recently, Reverend Childs has embraced a new spiritual practice—reading Scripture and reflecting on God's word through poetry and hymn lyrics inspired by the Psalms. He invites readers to journey through this collection of reflections, offering a heartfelt expression of God's powerful love. Through these writings, Reverend Childs hopes to inspire others and encourage a deeper connection to their own faith journey.

Made in the USA
Middletown, DE
26 May 2025